RECYCLING

RECYCLING

RE-USING OUR WORLD'S SOLID WASTES

BY JAMES AND LYNN HAHN

FRANKLIN WATTS, INC. | NEW YORK | 1973

Cover design by One + One Studio

Photographs courtesy of:
The Aluminum Association: pp. 19 (top and bottom), 43 (top and bottom), 44 (top and bottom); American Iron and Steel Institute: pp. 39, 40 (top and bottom), 50 (top and bottom), 54; Bergstrom Paper Company: 23, 24 (top and bottom), 27 (top and bottom); Glass Container Manufacturers Institute: pp. 11, 30, 32, 34, 35, 36; Lynn Lowery Hahn and James Sage Hahn: pp. 5, 8, 14 (top and bottom), 16.

Library of Congress Cataloging in Publication Data

Hahn, James.
    Recycling: reusing our world's solid wastes.

    (A First book)
    SUMMARY: Explains recycling, man's need of it, and present and suggested methods of performing the task for reusing waste materials.
    1. Salvage (Waste, etc.)–Juvenile literature. [1. Recycling (Waste)] I. Hahn, Lynn, joint author. II. Title.
TD792.H33   604'.6   73-4372
ISBN 0-531-00805-3

CONTENTS

**TO OUR
PARENTS**

Special thanks are due
Thomas J. Cunningham, Jr.,
W. P. Mahoney,
Hank Prehodka,
Emanuel L. Strunin,
Philip M. Tallmadge,
Bert Vorchheimer, and
Daniel J. Walsh
for their help
in furnishing
illustrative materials
for this book.

INTRODUCTION— MOUNTAINS OF TRASH, DUMPING, AND RECYCLING

A mountain of trash is beginning to bury the United States and other countries around the world. Every year the people in the United States throw away 50,000,000,000 food and drink cans, 27,000,000,000 glass bottles and jars, and 65,000,000 plastic and metal jar and can caps.

Ten thousand people produce enough garbage in one year to make a heap seven feet high covering a full acre. The entire population of the United States produces 3,500,000,000 tons of solid waste, such as bottles, cans, and plastic containers, every year. That means each person discards more than five pounds of trash each day.

The habit of throwing things away has created a huge garbage and rubbish disposal problem. And the mountain keeps growing. If people continue to throw things away at their present rate, the mountain of trash will double by 1987.

Over the centuries societies have developed several ways to dispose of trash and garbage. But none of these methods can cope with the enormous amount of rubbish produced today. City dumps, one of the oldest forms of waste disposal, are still the most common. About 85 percent of the garbage and trash collected in the United States is simply thrown into open dumps. Dumps are unpleasant to look at, create bad odors, poison water supplies, and cause disease problems by attracting rats, mosquitoes, flies, and other animals that carry disease-causing germs. And, as dumps keep growing, cities find they are running out of dumping space.

Garbage, paper, and cloth left in a dump for a long period of time will decay, break down, and be absorbed by the earth. Tin cans eventually rust and break up too, but the complete process takes about 100 years. Nature would take 400 years to break down aluminum cans left in dump heaps. Meanwhile the dump heaps get bigger and bigger as the population continues to produce more and more wastes.

Glass and plastic products present the worst dumping problems. Even over long periods of time, nature hardly affects them at all. Archaeologists have unearthed glass that was still in perfect condition after being buried more than 4,000 years in the trash heaps of past civilizations.

Enclosed burning, or *incineration,* solves some of the problems of dumping. It quickly reduces the volume of trash and garbage, but it still does not do away with nonburnables, such as aluminum and glass. The trash that does not burn must still be dumped somewhere. Some incinerators leave as much as 500 pounds of ash and nonburnables after burning one ton of garbage and rubbish. Incineration also pollutes the air with bad odors and with smoke and ashes that escape during burning. In some cases, the chemicals in the smoke can actually be poisonous to people's lungs, causing lung cancer and tuberculosis.

Dumping refuse into oceans and rivers is another form of waste disposal that pollutes our resources. Sometimes the rubbish simply floats back to shore, where it must be disposed of again. Other times it floats out to sea, forms stinking islands of pollution, and kills the fish, other animals, and plants that live in the ocean. A 20-square-mile area in the Atlantic Ocean has been so ruined by garbage and rubbish that marine life can no longer survive there.

This city incinerator
burns garbage and rubbish.

In some other areas, the fish do survive, but they carry poison in their bodies. If people eat these fish they may be poisoned too.

These methods of getting rid of waste not only cause pollution problems, they cost too much money. Every year, communities in the United States spend almost $5,000,000,000 to collect and dispose of solid wastes. Only schools and highways take a larger share of city budgets.

WHAT IS RECYCLING?

You, your family, and your friends can help to solve the garbage and rubbish disposal problem by taking part in a process called *recycling.*

Recycling simply means re-using things instead of throwing them away. Some things are still in perfect condition when they are recycled. Other things may have worn out in their original use, but they can be used to make something new.

The things we use can be recycled in so many ways that it would be impossible to list them all. Some of the ways of recycling things have not even been thought of yet. Every day individuals, communities, and industries find new ways to re-use materials that, only a few years ago or even a few days ago, they may have thought useless.

Some kinds of recycling require complicated mechanical processes. Industries use many machines to make new bottles from old bottles that have been crushed, or to make new paper from old, used paper that would otherwise be thrown away. Factories also use old bottles and old cans to make completely different materials. For example, they might use crushed glass as an ingredient in asphalt used to build a highway. Or they might use melted-down tin cans to make steel for new automobiles. Scientists constantly experiment to find new ways of using materials that people throw away.

A bag full of cans joins a load of newspapers
as this boy packs the family car for a trip
to the recycling center.

Sometimes, as with returnable soft drink bottles, recycling means re-using a container or material for its original purpose. Factories clean returnable bottles and refill them with fresh liquids. One bottle may be re-used from 14 to 20 times in this way.

Recycling can also mean finding new uses for something right in your own home. Empty coffee cans and empty plastic containers, for example, have outlived their original purpose, but they can be used for many new kinds of storage, or to build such things as birdhouses.

The idea of re-using things instead of discarding them is not new. If we look at nature, we can see that recycling has been going on for millions of years. Living things do not become waste when they die. Nature recycles them for new uses. Plants and animals that died millions of years ago underwent great heat and pressure to become coal that man uses as a valuable fuel. African elephants have long participated in a recycling process by shredding the bark and fibers of baobab trees. The shredded tree parts decay and their many minerals are recycled into the earth to enrich the soil for future plants.

Although they may not have used the term "recycle," people too have been re-using materials for centuries. For generations people have saved pieces of old clothing to use for cleaning and polishing rags, and to make fine quality papers. Automobile junkyard dealers have recycled parts of old wrecked cars for years. Although the car as a whole is no longer useful, the dealer can salvage such parts as bumpers, hub caps, tires, headlights, and numerous engine parts to be used again.

Even the idea of mechanically recycling things is not new. In 1800, Matthias Koops, an Englishman, received a patent from the British government for a process that took ink out of old paper and used the old paper to make new paper. Koops produced recycled paper more than 170 years ago, but no one in England seemed impressed enough to develop the process on a large scale.

YOU, RECYCLING, AND YOUR COMMUNITY

Today, communities, industries, and families *are* interested in the paper recycling process. They are interested in glass recycling, metal recycling, and any other process that can prevent our great junk heaps from growing bigger. When you take part in recycling, either in your home or in a community project, you are helping solve the problems caused by dumps, incinerators, and the dumping of garbage and rubbish into oceans.

By recycling you are also helping to save your natural resources. Every ton of paper that is recycled saves 17 trees from being cut down for new paper. Every piece of glass or metal that is recycled saves the earth from being stripped for the minerals that are used in new glass and metal.

You, your family, and your friends are the most important people involved in recycling. It is easy to see how you can recycle bottles, cans, and plastic containers in your own home by using them for storage or to make decorations, and to build things. You may have also recycled paper by making papier-mâché decorations or ex-

You're never too young to participate in the recycling operation. Here, a Brownie Scout has collected soft drink and other bottles to take to her collection center.

hibits for school. But did you ever stop to think that you are also the most important person in the complicated processes industry uses to recycle paper, glass jars and bottles, and aluminum and tin cans? If you throw these things away, they will probably be discarded with all the other trash in your community. Then the trash problem will never stop growing; more trees will be cut down for new paper; and more minerals will be taken from the earth to make glass and metal.

It is up to you, your family, and your friends to save bottles, jars, papers, and cans so they can be used to make new things.

Many communities help individuals to take part in recycling by sponsoring collection centers where people can take their cans, papers, and glass. In some communities, these centers are sponsored by groups of college or high school students, by Girl Scouts, Boy Scouts, and other young peoples' clubs, or by other groups of adults or children. Perhaps you or your parents belong to such a group.

Sometimes these groups pick up the materials at your home. They may also distribute information to help people learn more about recycling and waste disposal problems, and to tell you how to prepare your bottles, jars, cans, and papers for industrial recycling. Elementary schools in some communities sponsor drives to collect materials for recycling. Some school systems even award prizes to classes that collect large amounts of trash for recycling.

Some cities use recycling projects not only to keep their environment clean, but to provide jobs for people who might otherwise be unable to find work. One city has organized former drug addicts, men who have served prison terms, and men who are waiting for trial or sentence, to collect old newspapers for recycling. Some states are even considering using prisons as centers for collecting, cleaning, and processing materials for recycling.

PREPARING MATERIALS FOR RECYCLING

Before bottles, jars, cans, and even papers can be sent to recycling plants, they must be prepared for the recycling processes. Some collection groups prepare the materials themselves. But many communities and groups ask the people who save cans, glass, and papers to help. You can do most of the steps in preparing the materials yourself.

Wash out the cans, bottles, and jars, and take the paper labels off the cans. Some bottles have metal rings around their necks that helped seal the caps. Ask your mother or father to remove these with a small metal instrument such as an ice pick, screwdriver, or awl. If these metal rings are left on the bottles, they will form dark spots in the glass when it is melted during the recycling process.

Some communities ask that you smash the cans that are to be recycled. Use a can opener to remove both ends of the can. Place the ends inside the can, and step on the can to flatten it. All factories do not require that the cans be flattened, but flattened cans are easier for collection groups and communities to store and transport.

Finally, you can help sort the materials for recycling. If there is a collection center in your community, it probably provides separate bins for brown or yellowish-brown glass, green glass, and clear glass. Bottle manufacturers do not want different colors of glass to be mixed together, because the mixing would ruin the color of the

new glass. Scientists are developing new machinery to automatically sort old glass by color right at the glass-making factory. But until they perfect these machines, they must depend on your help.

Some communities and collection groups accept both tin and aluminum cans mixed together, but others ask the people to separate the two types of metal. Some collection groups accept only aluminum cans. Aluminum cans are easier to recycle than tin cans, because they are made of only one type of metal. "Tin" cans, such as soup or vegetable cans, are actually made of steel which is coated with tin on the outside, and may be coated with another metal on the inside. Another type of steel can, called a bi-metallic can, is all steel except for an aluminum end. Many easy-open beverage cans fall into this group.

Some communities collect only aluminum cans because aluminum manufacturers pay more for old cans than do iron and steel manufacturers. If your community asks you to separate the types of cans, you must learn their differences. Most aluminum cans contain beverages, such as beer and soft drinks. Aluminum cans are softer than steel cans, and can usually be pinched easily. Steel beverage cans have a side seam. Aluminum beverage cans do not. *Never* send aerosol spray cans, such as hairspray or furniture wax cans, to a recycling center. If heated, the aerosol cans might explode and seriously injure someone.

Like most city recycling centers in the United States, this one above provides separate bins for cans and for different colors of glass.

Obeying the signs at the recycling center below, a young recycler throws a green bottle into the correct bin. Lid and metal rings have already been removed.

Your community or collection group may also ask you to separate paper products for recycling. Some groups collect only newspapers, so you should see that other types of paper, such as magazines, are not mixed in with the newspapers. Other groups accept all kinds of paper. Any kind of paper can be recycled, unless it contains plastic. But, just as glass manufacturers do not mix different colors of glass, paper manufacturers do not mix different types of paper.

Some centers provide tools to prepare bottles for recycling. Here, a man uses a screwdriver to remove metal rings from the necks of bottles.

RECLAMATION CENTERS

After large amounts of materials have been collected, the community, collection group, or individual citizen takes the materials to places called *reclamation centers.* The paper, glass, and metal industries sponsor separate centers in various locations throughout the United States. Reclamation centers pay the cities and collection groups for the paper, glass, and metal, make final preparations for recycling, and send the materials on to recycling plants. Some private scrap dealers also buy used paper and metal and sell it to recycling plants.

Reclamation centers pay the most for aluminum wastes, such as aluminum cans and frames from old lawn chairs. Aluminum is very expensive to manufacture from new materials, so manufacturers are glad to have the chance to reuse old aluminum. In fact, about 30 percent of the aluminum in the United States has been recycled.

If there is no collection center or collection group in your community, you as an individual can still take part in glass, metal, and

Above, at an aluminum can reclamation center, each recycler is assigned his own bin for aluminum scrap, then awaits the next step in the recycling process.
Below, cans drop into a bin on an electric scale, which records the weight of the aluminum on a printed paper. Recycler then redeems paper for payment at the cashier's window.

paper recycling. Telephone or write to the glass, metal, and paper factories in your area to learn where the nearest reclamation centers or scrap dealers are located. If there are reclamation centers nearby, you and your parents can take your prepared bottles, jars, and papers directly to these centers. The centers will then pay you for the amount of trash you bring in.

You may also wish to help clean up your community by collecting bottles, jars, cans, and papers that other people have discarded. One young boy in the United States began collecting discarded glass and metal and selling it to reclamation centers when he was ten years old. In two years, he had earned $8,000 from his collections, while helping clean up his community. If there is no regular collection program in your area, you and your friends might wish to organize one with your church, scout troop, school, or other group.

A few communities in the United States collect material for recycling without using collection centers or collection groups. Several cities use electromagnets to separate iron and steel, including "tin" cans, from other garbage and trash. The electromagnet moves over the pile of trash and attracts the iron and steel items, pulling them out of the other rubbish. A few cities also employ workers to pick out glass, aluminum, and other nonmagnetic recyclable materials as the rubbish moves along a conveyor belt on its way to the incinerator.

One American city has a special waste treatment machine that separates materials for recycling. Bottles, jars, cans, and paper come to the machine mixed up with all the other garbage and trash from the city. A conveyor belt dumps the trash into a tub of water, with rotating blades like an airplane propeller at its bottom. Large heavy materials drop to the bottom of the tub and then pass under an electromagnet that collects iron and steel. The water containing the other materials then continues through a series of screens and other machines that collect glass, aluminum, other metals, and the wood fibers that make up paper. The city sells these materials to reclamation centers, and receives enough payment to cover half the costs of operating the machinery.

HOW PAPER IS RECYCLED

After glass, paper, and metal reach the reclamation centers, the materials must go through many more steps before they emerge as new bottles, jars, cans, paper, or other products. Let's look first at how the papers you save and collect are made into new papers.

Although Matthias Koops began to recycle paper in 1800, the process did not become common for another 100 years. Some paper manufacturers in the United States began recycling paper in the early 1900's. But even today, only about a fifth of the paper used in the United States is recycled.

Other countries recycle a much larger percentage of their paper. Almost half of Japan's paper is recycled. West Germany recycles almost a third of its paper, and Austria and the Netherlands recycle more than a third. About a fourth of the paper in Great Britain is recycled. Such countries as Canada, Denmark, Norway, and Sweden, which have large forests of trees suitable for making paper, usually recycle much smaller amounts.

Reclamation factories and scrap paper dealers take some steps in preparing paper for recycling before sending the paper to the paper mill. All waste paper is not of the same grade, so all types of paper cannot be mixed together for recycling. Cardboard and newspapers, for example, cannot be used to make high quality printing paper, but they can be used to make more cardboard and newspaper.

Factories sort the scrap paper products according to their quality and what they can be used to produce. Corrugated boxes and cardboard can be used to make new boxes, board, and wallboard. Old newsprint can be recycled for new newsprint, egg cartons, corrugated boxes, and wallboard. Mixed waste paper from offices, such as typing paper, note paper, and mixed envelopes can be recycled to make shoe boxes, cardboard tablet backs, and tar paper used in roofing. Glossy magazines, ledgers, index cards, and business machine papers can be recycled to high quality printing paper, paper cups and paper plates, food cartons, paper towels, and facial tissues.

After the paper has been sorted, the reclamation plant or waste paper dealer ties the different grades of paper into bales to be sent to the paper mills. Each bale may weigh as much as a ton. Every recycling plant does not use exactly the same procedure to make paper from used paper, but the basic steps are the same.

Let's follow some bales of high grade paper as they are used to manufacture new printing paper.

When the bales reach the paper mill, they are put on a conveyor belt and broken open. An inspector checks the opened bales to be sure nothing was packed in them by mistake. Sometimes the inspector must remove such things as broom handles, rags, bottles or metal tools. These materials could ruin the new paper.

The conveyor belt then moves the old paper to a huge machine, called a *hydrapulper.* Hot water in the hydrapulper cooks the paper until it forms a thick soup of wastepaper fibers. During this operation, detergent and chemicals, such as caustic soda, begin to remove old inks from the millions of tiny wood fibers that make up paper.

By this time, the old paper has become paper *pulp* that looks something like cottage cheese. It moves from the hydrapulper to special spinners. As the spinners whirl the pulp around, pins,

At this paper mill's storage warehouse, one-ton bales of waste and scrap paper await recycling.

staples, and other materials that might have been attached to the paper spin out of the mixture. From the spinners, the pulp goes to a series of moving screens that take out other impurities. A series of washers finish cleaning the pulp by removing ink, dirt, clay, and any starches or chemicals from the original paper.

After washing and screening, the pulp is clean, but it may not appear very white. It must be bleached with chlorine so that all the fibers become the same whiteness. Then the chlorine bleach must be washed out of the pulp, just as a washing machine must wash bleach out of your white clothes before they can be worn again. The pulp passes through more screens and spinners which remove any materials that weigh even a tiny bit more than the paper fibers. Then a vacuum cleaner sucks out some of the water to make the pulp thicker, and a final shower removes the last bits of dirt or other impurities left in the pulp.

Now the pulp is just as clean and white as new paper pulp, and it is ready to be made into paper. Some paper mills make paper entirely from recycled fibers. Others may use half recycled fibers and half new fibers, or some other combination of new and used pulp. The recycled pulp then moves to beating and mixing machines. If new fiber is to be added, it is first broken up in another hydrapulper. Then the mixing machine carefully blends the new and recycled fibers. After more beating operations, the pulp is pumped to the papermaking machines.

A huge box at the beginning of the papermaking machine slowly feeds the pulp onto a wire mesh that will begin forming the pulp

Above, waste paper moves into a hydrapulper,
which mixes and cooks it in hot water until
it becomes a thick soup. Caustic soda
and detergent are added to remove inks.
Below, the pulp, looking like cottage cheese,
moves through a series of washing operations
to remove impurities.

into sheets. The wire mesh looks somewhat like a huge moving window screen. A series of rollers keeps the 14-foot-wide mesh moving forward at a high rate of speed. As the pulp is fed onto the mesh, the mesh shakes from side to side. This pushes the paper fibers together and shakes some of the water out of the pulp. When the pulp begins its journey along the wire it is 99 percent water, and only 1 percent fiber. Gradually the water drains through the wire as the pulp continues on its long journey. The papermaking machine may be as long as a football field.

The wire mesh feeds the paper sheet into rollers that press together to squeeze out more water. Other machines suck out even more water before the paper sheet moves to dryer rollers.

The dryer rollers are heated to steam out the last drops of water. As the paper moves through the drying machine, clay and starches are applied to both sides of it. The clay and starches give the paper a smooth, hard surface for printing and writing.

Finally, the paper moves through more heated rollers that iron it smooth. The finished paper comes off the machine in three-ton rolls. The rolls are cut to whatever size the customer wishes and are wrapped and shipped to a printer or publisher. A finishing plant cuts the paper into small sheets for customers who do not wish to handle large rolls.

Some of the steps in recycling other grades of paper are different. For example, pulp for cardboard boxes or tablet backs does not need to be bleached, because it makes no difference whether the

Above, recycled waste paper pulp is pumped into the papermaking machine and spread across wire meshing. The machine, which is as long as a football field, later squeezes, rolls, and dries the pulp. Below, finished recycled paper comes off the machine in huge three-ton rolls.

fibers are all the same color. Lower grades of paper may not need to be washed so many times during pulping operations. But the basic steps of pulping, removing such things as staples and pushing fibers together on a papermaking machine, are common to all types of paper recycling.

Paper manufacturers say that the same paper can be recycled an endless number of times. However, some paper mills do not wish to recycle because they have difficulty selling the recycled paper. Many publishers, printers, and other companies that use large quantities of paper believe that paper fibers become weaker and shorter when they are recycled because the hydrapulper breaks them up. But paper recyclers claim that the recycling processes make the paper softer and easier to use. Paper recycling in the United States can expand only when the paper manufacturers and buyers resolve this problem.

Paper recycling is not limited to making paper from paper, or cardboard from cardboard. One United States factory recycles newspapers, gum wrappers, tissues, boxes, and books into paper tubes. It uses the tubes, combined with shiny flexible plastic parts, to build racks and shelves for hardbound and paperback books. Because it holds water so well, some people have used shredded waste paper to grow mushrooms.

HOW GLASS IS RECYCLED

Like the process of making paper from paper, the process of making glass from glass is not new. For many years, bottle manufacturers have used *cullet* (crushed glass) as an ingredient in batches of new glass. Using old glass saved the manufacturers money because they did not need to mine such large quantities of the chemicals needed to produce new glass. If the glass manufacturer makes new glass entirely from old glass, he can also save money on his glass furnace. Why? Because the furnace needed to melt old glass into liquid glass is much less complicated then the furnace needed to melt and blend all the dry ingredients used in new glass.

Manufacturers begin the process of making new glass from old glass by crushing the old jars and bottles into chunks of cullet. Huge machines do the crushing. The machines are completely enclosed so that no pieces of sharp glass can fly out and hurt any of the workers. When the machine is finished, the bits of cullet are small enough to slip through a hole less than ³/₄ of an inch in diameter.

Some companies and reclamation centers require that the bottles and jars be crushed before they are delivered to the company. Sometimes someone at the recycling center smashes the glass with a sledge hammer before it goes to the factory or reclamation center. But this is a job for adults only. The person who does it must be very careful not to get cut. The person should wear long sleeves,

gloves, a face mask, and safety glasses or goggles. Moreover, the glass should be crushed inside a metal can, so that it cannot fly off in all directions. A few recycling centers have small, enclosed grinding and crushing machines for recyclers to use. This eliminates the dangers of broken glass injuring someone.

At the bottle or jar-making factory, bucket elevators scoop up the cullet and move it to a special section of a tall storage silo. The silo may have other sections to hold silica sand, soda ash, limestone, and feldspar — the ingredients that make up the new glass. Some bottle manufacturers use about half cullet and half new ingredients to make one batch of glass. Some companies make new glass from cullet alone. The bottles and jars you use today may have been made partly or entirely from old glass. And you can help to see that these same bottles are used to make more new glass by recycling what *you* use.

At the bottom of the storage silo are huge weighing bins. When the glass factory is ready to make glass, cullet drops into one bin. If the cullet is to be mixed with other ingredients, each of those ingredients drops into its own bin. It takes thousands of pounds of each ingredient to make just the right combination of glass for jars and bottles.

After the glass ingredients have been weighed, they fall into a *batch mixer* that looks and works something like a huge cement mixer. The mixer tumbles the cullet and other ingredients until they become an evenly-mixed *glass batch*. The glass company may wish to store the glass batch for some time before using it to make glass.

Up until this point, the glass batch has been simply a mixture of dry ingredients. But now it is ready for the glass furnace. The glass furnace melts the cullet and other ingredients together to form a thick syrup. The furnace operates at 2,800° Fahrenheit; it is so hot

Workers deliver cullet *(crushed glass) to storage silos to await glass-making process.*

and bright that it would hurt your eyes to look into the mixture. The thick, syrupy glass flows out of the furnace into a device called an automatic feeder. The feeder cuts off the syrup in red-hot *gobs,* each one just large enough to make one bottle. One by one the feeder drops the gobs into a chute.

Each gob drops through the chute into a blank mold. A bottle-making machine blows a small bubble into the center of the gob. Then it blows the edges of the gob into the mold to shape the neck of the bottle or jar so that it can hold a cap or lid. When the top of the bottle or jar is finished, the hot, pliable gob moves to another mold, called a *blow mold.* While the gob is in the blow mold, the bottle-making machine blows more air into the bubble in the gob. It keeps blowing until the gob becomes the shape of a bottle or jar. After each recycled bottle or jar has been completely shaped, the mold opens and an automatic arm moves the container to a conveyor belt. At this point, the bottles and jars look finished, but they are not yet ready to be filled.

The conveyor belt carriers the recycled glass containers to an *annealing oven,* or *lehr.* The lehr slowly heats, then slowly cools the pieces of glassware as the conveyor belt moves them along. Slow heating and cooling helps give the glass overall strength so it will not break easily due to hot or cold temperatures.

When the bottles and jars come out of the lehr they are ready for use. A machine inspects them for imperfections. The factory workers inspect them for other defects. Imperfect bottles and jars cannot be used and are sent back to be crushed into cullet and recycled again. The manufacturer packs the perfect containers into shipping boxes and sends the boxes to warehouses. When a company needs bottles or jars in which to pack its products, trucks or trains bring it boxes full of containers.

Huge silos at glass making factory
store cullet and other ingredients
for making new glass.

*Left, as red-hot liquid glass flows out of the
furnace, automatic feeder cuts it into gobs.
Each gob is just large enough to make one jar
or bottle. Above, machine moves half-formed
bottle from neck-molding machine to another mold.*

Not all glass containers that are recycled are used to make more bottles or jars. Industries are always discovering new ways to use cullet. We have already seen how cullet can replace stones in asphalt, or "glasphalt" as the new mixture is called. It can also be ground up and used as a replacement for sand in cement, or even for sand on man-made beaches.

In addition, recycled cullet has been used instead of sand or stone in bricks, tiles, and sewer pipes. When cullet is used this way, it reduces the need for the quarrying of stone, which leaves ugly scars in our earth. Another use scientists have found for ground-up cullet is as a replacement for gravel in barnyards. Chickens eat the cullet and their systems use it to help them digest food because they do not have teeth.

Cullet is also used in the center strip on highways to help the strip reflect light. So used, it can be seen easily at night or during hazardous weather conditions. Some cullet has even been used in spun-glass insulation, the material that builders put between the costume jewelry. Melted-down cullet can even be used to make inner and outer walls of a house to keep out the heat in summer and retain it in winter. The list of ways in which recycled glass, whole and crushed, can be re-used is endless.

Last mold opens and an automatic take-off arm prepares to move finished recycled jar to a conveyer belt for packing.

HOW METAL IS RECYCLED

Just as glass can be recycled in many ways, so metal cans may also be recycled for a wide variety of uses. "Tin" cans are recycled for three main purposes — to make new steel, to make new tin, and to help in a process that takes copper from copper ore. And, as with other materials, science and industry continue to experiment to find new uses for recycled metals.

Steel companies may receive used cans from reclamation centers or from communities that use electromagnets to remove steel cans from other trash. The company may use huge pressing machines to smash the cans into compact bundles. Other scrap iron and steel, such as parts from cars, may also be smashed in the bundles of used cans. Then an electromagnet picks up the bundles and drops them into the steel-making furnace. In the furnace, the used steel is melted at more than 3,000° Fahrenheit to form a hot liquid. Batches of new molten steel may be added and mixed with the recycled material. The new recycled steel may be used to make new cans, or to make any number of a huge variety of steel products.

One problem steelmakers face in producing recycled new cans is that most used cans have other metals mixed in with the steel that may contaminate the fresh steel batch. These metals include aluminum ends, solder used in the side seams of the cans, tin outside coatings, and other inside coatings. If the aluminum ends are cut away from the cans before they go to a recycling plant, they

*This large electromagnet prepares
to drop bales of used cans into
an electric furnace for remelting
into recycled steel.*

will be separated from the cans by the electromagnet. Steel is attracted to magnets, aluminum is not. Some can-making companies are eliminating the problem of tin coatings by coating steel cans with a chromium and resin film instead. These materials mix with the steel better than tin, so they do not ruin the new steel batch when recycled.

Some plants use a detinning process to separate the tin coatings from steel cans before the cans are recycled. Detinning yields two recyclable materials — steel and tin. Detinners first run the cans through a shredding machine that cuts the cans into tiny strips, just as a kitchen grater cuts up cabbage. The shredded cans are added to a solution for a process called *electrolysis.* In electrolysis, an electric current runs through the solution and causes the tin to separate from the steel.

The United States has only a few small natural tin deposits, so detinning cans and recycling the metal is an important source of American tin. Other tin must be imported from foreign countries. Every year detinning companies recycle more than 600,000,000 used "tin" cans. Some metal companies say that the recycled tin is purer than new tin taken from ore.

The third major way "tin" cans are recycled is an important method of removing copper from copper ore, a process called *leaching.* In leaching, water with sulfuric acid in it is passed through the copper ore. The solution dissolves the copper from the ore. Then the solution is poured into vats full of shredded steel cans.

Above, this recycling machinery shreds steel cans and separates electrolytically the tin and steel materials for use in producing new steel and chemical products. Below, an overhead crane dumps untreated copper ore and shredded cans into a leaching vat; shredded cans help remove copper from the ore.

Because the iron in the cans is a more chemically active metal than copper, some of it dissolves and takes the place of the copper in the solution. Then the copper forms a deposit on the surface of the remaining can shreds. Later the copper manufacturer shakes and washes the shredded cans to remove the copper for refining.

Aluminum cans are recycled to make new cans. It takes about $126\frac{1}{2}$ used cans to make 115 new cans. At the reclamation center, the old cans pass through a magnetic separator. Since aluminum is not attracted to magnets, the magnet has no effect on the aluminum cans, but it removes any iron and steel mixed in with them. A huge rotary machine then cuts the aluminum cans into shreds the size of a dime. The machine is so powerful that it can cut a whole refrigerator into chunks no bigger than a fist. Trains carry the aluminum chips from the reclamation center to aluminum factories, where the chips are unloaded into hoppers.

A gas-powered aluminum furnace melts the chips into hot liquid metal. The furnace is so hot that it burns up any labels printed on the cans. From the furnace, the aluminum flows into molds to form *ingots,* or bars of metal. Workers take samples of the liquid metal to be sure it is of high quality. As the ingots harden, the workers skim off any impurities that rise to the top of the molds. After the ingots are hard, they are shipped to aluminum fabricating plants.

At the plant a series of rollers squeezes the aluminum into sheets just the right thickness to make cans. The long sheets are rolled into coils and are sent to manufacturing plants where the aluminum is shaped into cans.

Other metal products besides cans may also be recycled. Some

Above, at reclamation center, aluminum cans are placed in a hopper and carried on a moving belt through a magnetic separator that removes any steel cans. Below, a hammer mill or shredder chops the aluminum into dime-sized chips for melting in special furnaces.

aluminum reclamation centers accept clean scrap aluminum, such as frames from lawn chairs.

Discarded auto bodies present one of the greatest potential supplies of scrap metal in the United States. Each year the people in the United States discard 7,000,000 to 8,000,000 cars. But automobiles contain so many materials in addition to steel that recyclers are just beginning to consider them. A new electric steel furnace can melt down whole auto bodies for fresh steel, and a new "car-eater" machine that uses magnetic separation can reduce a car to fist-sized chunks of 98 percent steel in less than 60 seconds. Scientists have also discovered another use for auto bodies. Marine biologists use them as artificial reefs in the ocean. Tiny ocean animals attach themselves to the auto bodies, and marine biologists are able to study them.

Industries are also finding ways to remove lead from scrap metals. And almost half the copper and brass produced in the United States comes from used metals.

*Above, impurities are skimmed off
aluminum ingots as the metal hardens.
Below, ingots are moved into a
rolling mill where the metal is
changed into sheet suitable for
making recycled aluminum cans.*

RECYCLING OTHER MATERIALS

Although the metal, glass, and paper industries are the only organizations to sponsor community recycling processes, they are not the only industries involved in recycling. And metal, glass, and paper are not the only materials being recycled.

Rubber manufacturers are one of the principal recyclers in the United States. Every year 100,000,000 tires are discarded in America. It is cheaper for tire manufacturers to recycle their tires into new tires than to process new rubber. Tires and other old rubber products are divided into grades, just as papers are. But the rubber grading process is much less complicated than paper grading. The rubber manufacturer grinds the various grades and treats them with chemicals. Then the old rubber is processed into rubber sheets to be used in the manufacture of new rubber products. About 60 percent of the recycled rubber goes into the manufacture of tires.

Some manufacturers have combined another type of recycling with the recycling of tires. They crush discarded walnut shells and mix them into the rubber during processing. The shells enable the finished tires to grip the snow-covered or icy roads better than pure rubber tires.

Some rubber manufacturers use tire recycling to extract products from the rubber itself. Each ton of old tires contains 140 gallons of re-usable oil. One company does not make new tires from old tires, but it does use the old tires to produce carbon black — a principal ingredient in tires. Another company removes iron and steel from the tires. Ground-up tires have been used in asphalt to help it wear a longer time. Marine biologists also use tires as artificial reefs, just as they use automobile bodies.

Science and industry are just beginning to find ways to recycle plastics. For many years, plastics manufacturers have recycled plastic scraps left in the factory when toys, tools, containers, and other plastic products are produced. The factories melt down these scraps and use them in new plastic batches. One company found a new way to grind up used plastic milk bottles and recycle them into plastic drainage pipes. Another company recycles discarded plastic cups into plastic wine racks. These forms of recycling depend on one type of plastic being separated from other plastics and other kinds of trash. The manufacturers could not process a mixture of different plastic products. If this type of recycling is to succeed, plastic manufacturers must find a fast, mechanical way to separate different types of plastics.

But American scientists have found one way to recycle mixed plastics. They grind the plastics up and use them to replace sand in concrete. They call the new material "plastcrete."

One company in Japan has developed a system of recycling a mixture of old plastics into new plastic. The system begins by smashing together used plastic bottles and other containers, plastic bags, plastic pipes, and other plastic objects. The plastic pieces are washed and a magnet removes any pieces of iron or steel, such as wire closures, nuts and bolts, and caps that may have been smashed with them. Then the company melts the waste plastics together and forms the soft plastic into pellets (tiny balls). The pellets can be stored and later used to manufacture new plastic pipes and containers.

A factory in England has also developed a way to recycle mixed plastic wastes. The process shreds the plastics and feeds them into a machine that forms them into plastic sheets. Heat can form the plastic sheets into a wide variety of shapes. The process can recycle almost any kind of plastic, including squeeze bottles, biscuit packaging, and even vinyl-coated wallpapers. Depending on the types of original plastic used in the mixture, the new plastic sheet may be as tough as steel or as pliable as leather. Some of it is used in the form of plastic pallets to cushion materials and keep them from being damaged when they are picked up by a fork-lift truck.

Scientists are also considering using discarded plastic materials as a fuel. When plastic is burned, it gives off much higher heat than wood or paper. This heat could be used to burn other materials, or to heat homes, offices, and factories.

RECYCLING GARBAGE AND RUBBISH

Many people do not realize that even garbage can be recycled. Sometimes factories recycle the particular type of garbage they produce. For example, some canning companies process peach pits into charcoal. Other garbage is reused or recycled in combination with trash, and some is recycled by itself after such things as metal, plastic, rubber, glass, and paper have been removed for their own recycling processes.

Garbage recycling is one type of recycling that communities can do entirely by themselves. Many European communities have been recycling garbage much longer than communities in the United States.

In the United States, Canada, and Europe, sanitary landfill is one of the oldest and most common methods of re-using garbage and rubbish. It involves compacting wastes, spreading it on land, and covering it with more earth. Sanitary landfill can be used to add land along shorelines; to fill such areas as old quarries; to reinforce land that seems likely to slide or crumble; and to build ski slopes, soap box derby courses, or other hills in flat areas. When completed, landfill areas can be made to grow grass, trees, and other plants, and to support buildings. Part of Montreal, Canada's Expo '67 was built on landfill.

Landfill also provides a cheap, easy way for communities to get rid of their wastes while using them to make improvements in their

area. In its simplest form, it does not even require that the trash be sorted.

Communities use two basic methods of landfill — the area method, and the trench method. The area method simply involves filling and covering the area, such as a gully, quarry, or shoreline that is already lower than its surroundings, or building up an area to make an artificial hill. A tractor spreads the day's collection of waste, covers it with a six-inch layer of dirt, and smashes the dirt down to seal in the trash. When the landfill has risen as high as the community wishes, bulldozer tractors cover the entire area with a two- or three-foot layer of dirt. In the trench method, tractors dig a series of trenches, leaving walls of dirt between each trench. The community fills each trench with refuse. It then uses the dirt dug out of the trenches to cover and seal the filled trench.

Although sanitary landfill offers a cheap, easy way to re-use and get rid of trash and garbage, it can be only a very temporary solution. Eventually most communities can expect to run out of areas that can be used for landfill. New York City, for example, fills 200 acres a year and will run out of landfill space by 1975. Some cities must already ship their garbage to landfill areas in other cities. One United States city has slowed down the landfill process by squeezing its garbage and rubbish into tight, odorless little bundles

Above, this public collection truck is dumping its garbage into long receiving conveyor machinery which will shred it into reusable landfill. Below, this community's bulldozer is pushing just-delivered household garbage onto a conveyor belt that moves the garbage under a magnetic separator. Steel cans can thus be extracted for recycling and are moved into the truck trailer.

before using it for fill. A powerful press can compact 5,000 pounds of trash into a solid four-foot cube.

Other problems also limit the usefulness of sanitary landfill. If water stands on or flows over the landfill area, it must be kept away from community water sources, because it might pick up bacteria, fungus, or other harmful substances involved in decomposing the rubbish used in the landfill.

Another problem involves building on the filled areas. The landfill may continue to settle for several years while the fill decomposes. Heavy buildings need special, expensive foundations and architecture to withstand the settling. At the same time, the process of decomposing produces dangerous methane gas. If the gas rises only gradually to the surface of the fill and mixes with air, it causes no dangers. But it may concentrate in an enclosed building and cause an explosion.

Probably the worst problem with sanitary landfill is that it wastes valuable materials, such as glass and scrap metal. In landfills, these materials are re-used only once. But if they are separated for their own recycling process, they can be re-used a countless number of times. Some communities combine reclamation and landfill by first removing materials from the trash pile that can be recycled in other ways.

ENERGY FROM GARBAGE AND RUBBISH

Many cities around the world use garbage and rubbish for another purpose — to provide heat and electricity. Several European countries have been using it since the late 1940's. Communities in the United States have used this process, called *energy recovery*, for only a few years.

In energy recovery, garbage and rubbish are burned, and the steam and other hot gases produced by the burning are used to generate electricity or to power a heating plant. When burned, a city's garbage has about one-third the heating power of an equal amount of coal. Since it is more readily available than coal, and must be disposed of anyway, it makes a practical source of energy for cities and some industries. Garbage supplies a large portion of the heat and power for Paris, France; Montreal, Canada; and several cities in the United States.

As with all recycling processes, the exact steps each city uses in energy recovery are not all alike. For example, some systems separate metal and glass during the process, and some do not. Most systems start with a shredder that crushes, cuts, and mixes the garbage and rubbish so that all its pieces become the same size. The shredder is powerful enough to chop up tree logs or crush and shred refrigerators.

The shredding operation helps the bits of refuse to burn evenly. Left whole, a log would not burn as rapidly as a bag of paper cups.

This uneven burning could cause the heat or electricity supply to speed up while the paper cups are burning, and slow down while the log is burning. But when the different materials are shredded and mixed, they can burn at a more even rate and thus provide heat and electricity at an even rate. Some industries have systems that automatically classify materials according to the amount of heat they produce.

After shredding the refuse, some energy recovery systems send it through an air classifier. The air classifier consists of a stream of air that shoots through a zig-zag tube. The stream of air forces most of the garbage to continue on to a storage container. But heavy particles, such as glass and metal, fall out a hole in the bottom of the tube. Then they can be recycled separately. The wastes other than glass and metal continue on from the storage container to an incinerator, where they are burned. The hot gases that escape from the refuse during burning power a turbine, which is something like a propeller, which in turn drives an electrical generator. The system can burn 400 tons of waste every day, producing about 15,000 kilowatts of electric power. Some office buildings use electricity generated in this way to power their heating and air-conditioning systems.

Sweden has developed an especially efficient waste disposal system that is now being combined with energy recovery systems in many other countries, including France, Venezuela, Denmark, Japan, Germany, and the United States. The Swedish system uses a series of chutes and underground pipelines to carry waste to special incinerators. The chutes begin in apartment buildings, where residents simply open a small door in the wall and drop their garbage and rubbish down the chute. The underground pipe sucks the garbage down and moves it to the incinerator, which can produce heat to warm the building's water and provide heat in the winter.

This garbage will soon be removed in shredded form by the long conveyor to be used for much-needed landfill.

RECYCLING GARBAGE BY COMPOSTING

One method of recycling garbage has been popular in Europe for many years, but it is just beginning to be considered in the United States. The method, called *composting,* offers a way of recycling any organic materials — materials that are, or once were, alive. Composting factories expose the matter to air and water so that it will begin to decompose. Even old Christmas trees can be shredded and used for compost.

The compost makes a good soil conditioner, because it holds moisture in the soil. It is especially useful for growing crops that need very moist soil, such as mushrooms. Communities can use compost as landfill to reclaim the soil in such areas as coal strip mines, and to build up sliding embankments on the edges of roads. Compost also has a small value as a fertilizer because it contains nitrogen, phosphate, and potassium, the most important elements in fertilizer. Some communities use sewage sludge — the waste water from sewage treatment plants — to make compost more valuable as a fertilizer. A few communities in the Soviet Union recycle sewage alone as a fertilizer.

Many farmers and home gardeners have used the technique of composting for generations. They throw weeds, leaves, grass cuttings, and other plant matter onto a heap and allow it to decay. When the wastes have decayed, they spread them over their soil to help hold in moisture. City composting plants employ mechanical methods to make the compost more uniform. First they separate the organic and inorganic wastes and grind up the organic wastes. Then they allow the waste to decompose and dry. Finally, they screen the compost.

Compost plants use two main methods of treating garbage. One method is similar to the farmer's way of composting. The garbage is piled in long rows on the ground or on a paved area. During the first week, workers turn it twice. Then the material is left to decompose for some period of time. There is no exact amount of time for the compost to decompose, because some materials, such as leather, heavy paper, and wood chips, take longer than others to break down.

The other method of composting uses mechanical processes to speed the job. The organic material is placed in a tank that either revolves or has air blown through it to turn and dry the garbage. The material stays in the tank for five to seven days, then it is taken out to cure.

One of the main objections in the United States to both methods of composting is that they are rather expensive. Both methods require large areas of land — from five to 30 acres for a small city — and the equipment used in mechanical composting is also expensive. In the United States, too, few people want to buy compost because chemical fertilizers are cheaper. And so, American cities have a difficult time selling enough compost to cover the costs of producing it.

RECYCLING IN THE FUTURE

The range of other types of recycling presently being experimented with, or just being thought of, is so wide that only a few of them can be mentioned here. Scientists are experimenting with chemical and mechanical ways to recycle garbage and trash to save their most useful products. For example, one experimental method takes sugar from wool, paper, and other wastes. And scientists in China have produced more than 50 products from the waste water and other waste materials produced by chemical industries.

Another method that is still in the experimental stage is called *pyrolysis*. Pyrolysis plants heat waste materials to 1000° Fahrenheit or more in an atmosphere of very little oxygen. The process breaks down the wastes to about 10 percent of their original size, while removing such useful products as gas, tar, oil, and other chemicals. Pyrolysis of some types of plastics produces a hard wax that can be used in polishing pastes and printing inks. A pyrolysis plant would take up about the same amount of space as an incinerator, but would not pollute the air as much as an incinerator. As with other recycling processes, recyclers must find a market for the materials they recover before they decide whether pyrolysis is profitable.

Today many scientists are experimenting with ways to provide new building materials through recycling. They have suggested using the waste or slag from blast furnaces in the steelmaking process to replace stone in road building. The United States government has used a paving material made from trash and garbage to resurface roads and parking lots in an airport. Some scientists are working with the slag from coal ash production to make an insulating material for buildings. Others are working on a method to compress wastes into rockhard blocks, and then coat the blocks with asphalt or cement for building. Japan has already used blocks made from garbage to reclaim parts of Tokyo Harbor.

Some of the recycling methods suggested for the future deal with materials that are already being recycled in some form right now. Old or abandoned automobiles, for example, may be run through a giant hammermill that can chop the iron and steel into shreds the size of gravel and sand. The scrap could then be used in road beds. Recyclers expect future car manufacturers to design vehicles so "car-eater" machines can easily break them up to make new iron and steel. Various manufacturers are also expected to make many more of their car parts interchangeable with the other parts on other makes of cars. If this is done, more pieces of scrap autos can be used to replace damaged or worn-out parts on autos that are still in use.

Scientists are experimenting with ways to burn rubber tires, and then to use the solid wastes therefrom as filters for sewage treatment plants. At least one scientist has developed a building material made from cow manure and old glass. Bricks and planks made from this material will not burn, will not soak up water, and can be painted, glazed, drilled, nailed, glued, and sawed like wood. Scientists are also studying ways to use atomic power to quickly process garbage into crude oil and iron ore. And some researchers are even studying ways to recycle garbage into food. Indeed, industries have already recycled some garbage for use as animal food.

Furthermore, some scientists are working on ways to do away with the need to recycle large quantities of material. They are developing bottles that will disintegrate after long exposure to water, and a self-destructing plastic that crumbles when it is exposed to sunlight for long periods of time. They have also invented

a package for instant soup that dissolves in water right along with the soup. True, these methods help solve the trash problems, but they still waste resources because the containers are only used once. Some states are now considering laws to ban or tax throw-away containers so that people will be sure to return or recycle glass and metal containers.

Scientists, industries, governments, and concerned groups of citizens work every day to find new and better ways of recycling, and to teach people to use the methods of recycling that are available.

At present, many communities have no recycling centers; many people do not know about recycling; and many more never take part in the recycling projects going on in their communities. Meanwhile, the trash and garbage heaps around the world continue to grow; whole forests of trees continue to be cut down for paper; more valuable minerals are taken from the earth; and insufficient methods of waste disposal continue to pollute our beautiful planet.

Recycling our waste materials cannot solve all of these problems, but it *can* help. And the most important person in the whole process is *YOU.*

Even powerful bulldozers like this can't
solve the world's waste-disposal problem.
YOU can help in your own community by becoming
active in a recycling program.

A RECYCLING GLOSSARY

Air Classifier. A waste disposal machine consisting of a stream of air that forces garbage into a storage container. Heavy waste materials, such as glass and metal, fall out of a hole in the bottom of the air classifier and are recycled separately. Other waste materials are forced into an incinerator. The hot gases that escape from these burning wastes power turbines, which drive electrical generators.

Annealing Oven (also called **lehr**). An oven used in the glass-making process which slowly heats, then slowly cools glass pieces as a conveyor belt moves them along. Slow heating and cooling helps give the glass an overall strength so it will not break easily when exposed to hot or cold temperatures.

Baling. A recycling process where waste materials, such as used newspapers, are compacted into bundles held together with wire.

Biodegradable. Waste material capable of being broken down by bacteria into basic elements. Most wastes which are or once were alive, such as food remains and paper, are biodegradable.

Collection Center. A facility designed to accept waste materials from individuals, families, or groups. These facilities usually have space to store glass bottles and jars, metal, and waste paper.

Composting. Method of recycling any organic materials (materials that are or once were alive). The organic material is exposed to air and water so bacteria can begin to break down the wastes.

Cullet. Recycled glass, usually broken into small, uniform pieces about the size of a pea.

De-Inking. A process in paper recycling that uses detergents and chemicals, such as caustic soda, to remove old inks from the millions of tiny wood fibers in used paper.

Detinning. A process in can-recycling that separates tin and steel. The recycled cans move through a shredding machine that cuts the cans into tiny strips like a kitchen grater cuts up cabbage. Then the shredded cans are added to a chemical solution and prepared for electrolysis. In electrolysis, an electric current passes through the shredded steel and chemical solution, forcing the tin to separate.

Dump. An open land site where waste materials are burned, left to decompose, rust, or simply remain. The burning of waste materials in a dump generates smoke fumes and ash particles. Dumps can cause water pollution, and attract flies, rats, and mosquitoes.

Energy Recovery. A recycling process where a part or all of the waste materials entering a recovery facility are burned to produce heat, which can be used to produce steam for heating or for the generation of electricity.

Garbage. Waste materials which decompose easily, such as food wastes from kitchens and grocery stores, or wastes from slaughter houses and food processing plants.

Glasphalt. A material used in highway construction made with recycled glass that has been crushed and added to asphalt.

Hammermill. A machine that breaks waste materials into smaller pieces by using a system of heavy moving hammers.

Hydrapulper. A machine used in the papermaking process, which cooks used paper until it forms a thick soup of wastepaper fibers, called pulp. This machine also cleans the wastepaper by removing ink and other foreign materials.

Incinerator. A large furnace that burns waste materials. Most incinerators pollute the air and waste valuable materials, such as paper, plastic, and wood. In a few incinerators, the heat generated is used to produce steam and electricity for energy recovery.

Leaching. A process in metal recycling where "tin" cans help remove copper from copper ore. Water with sulfuric acid passes through copper ore. This chemical solution is then poured into vats full of shredded steel cans. Because the iron in the cans is a more chemically active metal than copper, some of the iron dissolves and takes the place of copper in the chemical solution. Next, the copper forms a deposit on the surface of the remaining shreds. Later, the copper manufacturer shakes and washes the shredded cans to remove the copper for refining.

Lehr. Also called an annealing oven (see definition on page 62).

Nonreturnable. Glass containers, such as bottles and jars; metal containers, such as beer and pop cans; and such plastic "bottles" as bleach and milk containers, which do not have any money deposit, are easily disposed of, and can be used only once unless they are recycled.

Plastcrete. A material used in concrete that can replace sand, and is made from recycled plastic.

Pulp. A material used in the papermaking process. Pulp can be obtained from wood fibers, or from wastepaper that has been cleaned and treated in the hydrapulper.

Pyrolysis. A recycling process that breaks down burnable waste by combustion in the absence of air. High heat is usually applied to the wastes in a closed chamber, evaporating all moisture and breaking down materials into various gases and solid residue. The gases are collected, used, and sold. The residue can be further processed into useful materials, or it can be used in a landfill.

Reclamation Center. A place sponsored by glass, metal, and paper industries where individuals or groups may bring materials for recycling and receive payment for these materials.

Recycling. Re-using waste materials to produce materials that may or may not be similar to the original.

Refuse. A general word for solid waste.

Returnable. Containers on which a deposit is paid, and which may be returned to the store to be re-used for their original purpose. The customer receives a refund when returning the containers.

Rubbish. Mixed waste materials, such as garbage and trash.

Sanitary Landfill. A method of disposing of wastes by spreading them over land, and covering the wastes with a seal of earth. Communities often use landfill to re-use wastes — to help fill low areas, or to build recreational facilities.

Trash. Waste materials other than garbage.

Waste Materials. Solid materials, or liquids in containers, which are discarded as worn out or worthless. Recycling permits the re-use of these discarded materials.

Wood Fiber. Tiny strands of material that can be reclaimed from old paper to make new paper. These strands make up the basic material in paper pulp.

| INDEX |